PRAISE FOR OTHER BOOKS BY
KEN WHITING AND ALEX MATTHEWS

"The sheer joy and sharp technique in your books and videos has everything to do with both our progress in learning and our happiness in achieving."
George Baldwin

"Thanks for creating such excellent instruction on kayaking."
Gary Bodnar

"A fantastic complement to any kayaker's library."
Eugene Buchanan, Editor, Paddler Magazine

"The Heliconia Press is clearly committed to producing the most detailed, concise and entertaining instructional products on the market."
Richard Parkin, Editor, Paddles Magazine

"Terrific instruction!"
Philippe Doux, Editor, Kayak Session/Paddle World Magazine

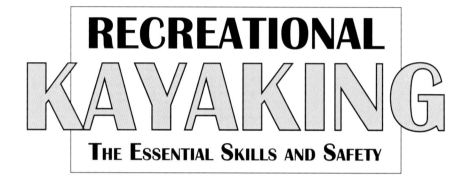

RECREATIONAL KAYAKING

THE ESSENTIAL SKILLS AND SAFETY

**BY ALEX MATTHEWS
AND KEN WHITING**

THE **HELICONIA PRESS**

Published by

 THE **HELICONIA PRESS**

1576 Beachburg Road
Beachburg, Ontario
K0J 1C0
www.helipress.com

This book was printed in Canada by Custom Printers, Renfrew, Ontario.

First Edition

ISBN # 1-896980-23-6

Written by: Alex Matthews and Ken Whiting
Photography by: Rob Wilson, Steve Metcalf,
Paul Villecourt and Jock Bradley,
except as noted.
Illustrations by: Paul Mason
Design & Layout: Robyn Hader
Editor: Jane Karchmar

About Safety

Kayaking is an activity with inherent
risks, and this book is designed as a
general guide, not a substitute for formal,
professional instruction. The publisher
and the authors do not take responsibility
for the use of any of the materials or
methods described in this book. By
following any of the procedures described
within, you do so at your own risk.

Library and Archives Canada Cataloguing in Publication

Matthews, Alex, 1964-

   Recreational kayaking : the essential skills
   and safety / by Alex Matthews and Ken Whiting.

ISBN 1-896980-23-6

   1. Kayaking. 2. Kayaking--Safety measures. I. Whiting, Ken, 1974-
   II. Title.

GV783.M382 2006   797.1'224   C2006-900277-0

Photo courtesy of Innova Kayaks

TABLE OF CONTENTS

ACKNOWLEDGEMENTS

Although technology continues to make book publishing easier, it hasn't impacted our reliance, as publishers and authors, on the help of others. A heartfelt thanks goes to all those that helped make this book possible.

First and foremost, I would like to thank Alex Matthews for sharing his passion and incredible knowledge of paddlesports.

Special thanks go to our wonderful designer, Robyn Hader, for her commitment to perfection; Lisa Utronki, Rob Wilson, Jock Bradley, Paul Villecourt and Steve Metcalf for their great photography; Kerry Thompson and the Custom Printers crew for making the whole printing process so enjoyable; Ruth Gordon for putting aside her whitewater paddle to help make this book happen; Joe and Sue Kowalski for making time for us and for their commitment towards preserving the wilderness in the Ottawa Valley, where much of the book was shot; Jane Karchmar; and Cindy Jamieson, Lindsey and Dylan Spencer, and Brent and Nadine Cooper for their willingness to strike a pose.

A sincere thank you also goes out for the ongoing and much appreciated support from Craig Langford and Joe Matuska of Aquabound, Sara Knies and Chris Jacobs of Ocean Kayak and Old Town, Andrew Sterling of Confluence, and Lisa, Martha, and Michael of Kokatat.

Finally, thanks to the THP crew for their commitment and dedication and for making every day in the office a pleasure.

INTRODUCTION

"Kayaking." For many, the word may conjure images of extreme sport. You might envision a testosterone-driven daredevil charging through raging river rapids. Some folks immediately focus on their fear of being sealed in a boat, flipping, and then feeling trapped underwater. Others will hear the word "kayak" and picture a fur-clad Inuit hunter in an elegant sealskin boat, stealthily gliding through the icy waters of an arctic sea.

In reality, kayaking is the most approachable, straightforward, and "user-friendly" way that I've ever encountered to get out on the water. I take immense pleasure in dispelling people's apprehension about getting into a kayak for the first time, because the truth is that kayaking is easy and it's truly for everyone. It's for kids, teens, adults, and seniors. It's for families, couples, or single individuals. A kayak, and paddling, is an amazing platform for getting outside and spending time with your friends and loved ones, and it's a great way to meet new people, too. Paddling is so much more enjoyable than spending time in a gym, and it's an exciting and active way to go fishing, bird watching, or exploring your local waterways. Kayaking can be so many different things to so many types of people, and make no mistake: kayaking is for everyone!

This book is about "recreational kayaking"--a very broad term that refers to paddling in kayaks that are typified by their compact size, focus on general performance, ease of use, stability, and overall fun. Recreational kayaks fall into two basic categories: "sit-on-top" kayaks (in which there is no enclosed space) and "sit-inside" kayaks (in which the paddler sits within the boat). While rec boats have been around for a long time, they have become more and more popular over the past few years thanks to refinements in design that have made the boats more user-friendly and more comfortable than ever. This has made it possible for virtually anyone to hop into a kayak for the first time and have fun without the need for any previous boating experience. Recreational kayaks also provide an ideal gateway to other forms of kayaking, such as sea kayaking, whitewater kayaking, kayak fishing, and surf kayaking.

Although recreational kayaking is a remarkably safe sport, any time you are interacting with a water environment, whether swimming, surfing, boating, or paddling, there is always some inherent risk. The fact that you're reading this book means that you're interested in learning more, and that's a great start. Understand, though, that a book or video is limited in its ability to effectively pass on skills and knowledge; as your confidence grows and you start to spread your kayaking wings, it is important that you consider formal instruction. Being able to swim is also one of the most basic skills that you can have to improve your safety factor while paddling.

With all this said, let me introduce Recreational Kayaking, and congratulate you for being one of the remarkably few people in this world who will step into, and take advantage of, the magical world of kayaking. I'm sure you'll find that on the days you paddle, the world is a little bit brighter.

ABOUT THE AUTHORS

ALEX MATTHEWS

Alex Matthews is a whitewater paddler, kayak-surfer and passionate sea kayaker. He has guided sea kayak trips in many areas around Vancouver Island, the Queen Charlotte Islands, and Baja, Mexico. He has explored sections of both the West and East Coasts of Canada and the United States. A successful writer known for his irreverent wit and humor, his articles have appeared in many prominent paddlesports publications, and he has worked in both kayak design and marketing for prominent paddlesport companies.

His abiding fascination for any liquid environment in general and the ocean in particular fuels his zeal for crafts that interact with water as directly as possible. It is no surprise that his Zodiac sign is Pisces – the fish.

KEN WHITING

After winning the World Freestyle Kayaking Championships in 1997, Ken focused his passion for paddling on the development of instructional tools. Ken is now one of the most influential paddlers in the world, and was recognized as such by *Paddler Magazine* as one of their "Paddlers of the Century." He has paddled on over 200 rivers in fifteen countries and has ten best-selling, award-winning instructional books and DVDs to his name. Ken and his wife, Nicole, live in Beachburg, Canada, where they run their publishing business, The Heliconia Press. For more information, visit www.helipress.com

CHAPTER ONE

EQUIPMENT

YOUR BODY • KAYAKS • PADDLES • PFDS
DRESSING TO GO KAYAKING • SAFETY EQUIPMENT • CHECKLIST

YOUR BODY

Although kayaking can be an incredibly low-impact sport, and you really don't need to be in great shape to enjoy it, you do need to be kind to your body. After all, it's the engine that powers your paddle and drives your boat, so you need to keep it running smoothly.

As with any physical activity, it's important to take the time to allow your body to warm up, so resist the urge to sprint away from the beach at full throttle. Of course, a stretching routine is also a great idea. Don't forget to stretch your lower body as well as your upper body. Tight hamstrings are one of the biggest reasons paddlers experience discomfort when kayaking. Because the seating position in a kayak places your legs out in front of you, tight hamstrings will make sitting up straight difficult, and will limit your ability to take full strokes.

Stretching your hamstrings will go a long way towards making the time spent sitting in a kayak more comfortable.

KAYAKS

Although there are many different forms of kayaking, this book focuses on recreational kayaking. Recreational kayaks, or "rec boats," are, by definition, the easiest boats to paddle, requiring no specialized nautical knowledge to operate or enjoy. Rec boats come in two basic formats: singles (for one occupant) or tandems (for two people). There are also two basic, self explanatory styles: "sit-on-top" and "sit-inside" kayaks. Both sit-on-top and sit-inside kayaks are available as hard shell boats and as inflatables. Hard shells are generally more popular, as they require no set-up. Inflatable kayaks are great, though, as they are versatile and much easier to transport when they've been deflated.

1. Sit-on-top
2. Sit-inside
3. Inflatable sit-on-top

Although sit-on-top and sit-inside kayaks have some differences, they share many of the same parts. The top of a kayak is referred to as the deck. The bottom is the hull. The front of the boat is called the bow, and the back is the stern. On deck, you'll often find deck lines for securing extra equipment like water bottles or sunscreen. Convenient carrying handles are located at both the bow and stern, and some kayaks have perimeter lines that make grabbing the boat easier still. Some also have rudders or skegs that help maneuver or keep the boat running straight (although neither are essential pieces of equipment). Rudders swivel side to side in the horizontal plane and are controlled by foot-pedals. Skegs are fixed along the centerline of the kayak and simply drop into the water to help the boat go straight. Sit-on-top and sit-inside kayaks both have seats and some forms of support for the feet, and the better models have built-in backrests.

Unique to sit-inside kayaks is the cockpit—the area within the boat where you sit. Around the cockpit you'll find the cockpit rim, otherwise referred to as the coaming. This raised lip allows a spraydeck to be attached to the boat in order to keep water out. Inside a sit-inside kayak are foot pedals that can be adjusted to accommodate paddlers with different leg lengths. While some sit-on-top kayaks use foot pedals too, many have foot wells instead. These recesses are molded right into the boat and the paddler simply places his/her foot in the most appropriate well for the length of the leg. Foot wells provide a slick and effective means for fitting different paddlers without the need for making any adjustments.

Choosing a Kayak

Recreational kayaks come in almost every length imaginable, so it's easy to get overwhelmed when trying to decide on what kayak is best for you. Take heart, though, as the decision does not need to be a difficult one. Recreational kayaks are all designed to make paddling fun and easy, so it's extremely unlikely that you'll

How you use your kayak plays the biggest role in dictating which is the best one for you.

make a wrong decision. The best way to narrow down your options is by clearly identifying how and where you'll be using your kayak, and then deciding on a rough budget for the purchase.

Your first and biggest decision is whether to go for a "sit-on-top" or a "sit-inside" kayak, and there are pros and cons to both. Sit-on-tops provide the ultimate in user-friendliness. Since you sit right on top of the kayak, your legs are totally free (although you can opt to use thigh straps that allow you to grip the kayak with your legs) and there is no feeling of confinement that sometimes accompanies a sit-inside. Sit-on-tops are also "self-bailing," meaning that water automatically drains out of the seat and foot wells through "scupper" holes that go right through the kayak. Their inherent stability also makes them very safe and fun to use. In fact, they are so easy to get into that you that you can slip on and off them as the urge takes you. If you do completely capsize, they don't even require emptying out--just flip them upright and scramble aboard! All these features make sit-on-top kayaks great for nervous paddlers, for paddling in warm environments, and for paddling in surf zones where flipping is a very distinct possibility.

Although these are some pretty compelling reasons to choose a sit-on-top kayak, there are also some great reasons to choose a sit-inside kayak. In fact, one of the sit-on-top's strengths is also its greatest weakness. The fact that you're not enclosed in any way when using a sit-on-top means that to paddle a sit-on-top is to be wet. On the other hand, sit-inside kayaks allow you to stay far drier and protect your lower body from the wind. The option of using a spraydeck further increases a paddler's defense against the cold and wet. For this reason, sit-inside kayaks are very popular in areas where both warm water and hot air temperatures aren't the norm. Like sit-on-tops, recreational sit-inside kayaks are generally very stable and easy to use. They also have large cockpits that minimize any possible feelings of confinement, and offer easy entry and exit from the boat. A final advantage of the sit-inside kayaks is that they are typically available in a wider variety of materials, which we'll explore in more detail in the next section. The downside of the sit-inside kayaks is that you don't have the same freedom to hop in and out of them while on the water, and, more importantly, recovering from a capsize is not a simple process. Because sit-inside kayaks are not self-bailing, capsizing will result in a swamped boat, which is very cumbersome to deal with. Some sit-inside kayaks have built-in flotation created by "bulkheads," which are waterproof walls on the inside of the kayak that divide the boat's interior into separate compartments. These compartments are accessed through hatches on the deck, and not only do they generate valuable flotation in the case of a capsize, they also provide a relatively dry spot for carrying gear.

Once you have decided on whether to go for a sit-on-top or sit-inside kayak, there are a few other issues to consider. As a general rule, the longer and narrower a boat is, the faster it will be. However, the wider a boat is, the more stable it will become, so narrower isn't necessarily better. Another factor to consider is that shorter boats are much easier to handle in transport and weigh considerably less than long ones--an important consideration for those who will routinely be hauling boats on their own or loading kayaks up onto high vehicles.

Rocker refers to the curvature of the kayak's hull, from bow to stern, as viewed from the side. The more rocker a boat has, the easier it will turn, but the less effectively it will hold a line, or "track." Most rec kayaks have very little rocker to ensure that they track well and are easy to paddle in a straight line. With this said, if your goal is to play in surf where maneuverability is a key issue, you'll want to choose a kayak with a larger amount of rocker.

What are kayaks made from?

Kayaks can be manufactured from a wide variety of materials. Most rec boats are made of rotomolded polyethylene, or "Tupperware," and there is good reason for this. Poly boats are amazingly affordable, incredibly durable, and perform very well, while requiring the absolute minimum of maintenance or care. You can also get kayaks made from "composites" like fiberglass, Kevlar© or carbon, which use resin and woven fibers to create their structure. Composite construction produces beautiful, lightweight parts that are stiff and glossy, but unfortunately they do not handle impact well, nor do they tolerate much abuse. They are also very expensive and are most suited to paddlers who want the highest performance and are willing to take

extra care with a significantly more fragile boat. Thermoformed boats are relatively new to the market and are becoming more and more popular. The material used in the thermoforming process provides a great-looking kayak that falls somewhere between composites and polyethylene with regards to durability, affordability, and weight. Inflatable kayaks are made from coated fabrics. While care should be exercised around sharp objects, the best inflatables are far more durable than most paddlers would imagine. Their compact dimensions when deflated also make inflatable kayaks ideal for folks who have limited space, or those who wish to transport their boats by airplane, train, or backpack.

PADDLES

ABOUT PADDLES

The paddle is your intimate connection between kayak and water. Kayak paddles come in a wide variety of shapes, sizes, and price ranges, so choosing one can be a daunting task. For casual paddling, however, any paddle that is durable enough to stand up to the abuse it will undoubtedly receive, and that will effectively propel your kayak forward, will likely be perfectly adequate. Of course, a good quality paddle does have real benefits. For instance, although a really lightweight paddle will cost more, it will make your time on the water more comfortable and even more enjoyable. This price versus performance issue only really becomes important as your outings get longer and more involved. Let's take a quick look at the options that are out there.

Paddles vary in length from 6.9 feet to 8.2 feet, and have three main parts to them. They have a shaft, a power face, and a back face. The power face is the side of the paddle blade that catches water when you take a forward stroke. Kayak paddles are made from a variety of materials, although for casual paddling, plastic and fiberglass are by far the most common, as they offer a great blend of performance, durability, and affordability.

When choosing a paddle, the two most important factors that you'll need to consider are its length and blade size. Your physical size and the width of your kayak will play the largest roles in your decision-making process. As a general rule, a smaller paddler should use smaller blades, while a stronger paddler can control a paddle with larger blades.

Similarly, it will be easier to use a longer paddle for a wider kayak, while shorter paddles are more appropriate for narrower kayaks.

A final decision you'll need to make has to do with the feather, or offset, of your blades. The feather is the amount of twist between the blades of a paddle. The

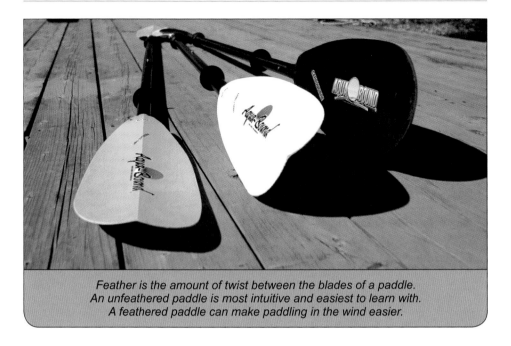

*Feather is the amount of twist between the blades of a paddle.
An unfeathered paddle is most intuitive and easiest to learn with.
A feathered paddle can make paddling in the wind easier.*

advantage of having blades that are offset is that in a headwind, the top blade slices through the air with minimal air resistance. On the other hand, a paddle with no offset is much more intuitive and a great option for most paddlers. One nice thing is that most recreational kayaking paddles come as two-piece designs and provide the option of being assembled with or without offset blades. There is no "right way" here, just personal preference.

Paddle leash

A paddle leash attaches your paddle to you or to your boat so that if you drop your paddle, you don't need to worry about losing it. Leashes are great when taking photos, fishing, or in the event of a wet exit. It may sound hard to believe, but without a leash, even in broad daylight and calm conditions, it can be surprisingly difficult to spot and retrieve a paddle that has floated only a short distance away.

PFDS

PFDs (Personal Flotation Devices) are the single most important piece of safety equipment and should always be worn when on the water. A PFD should have a number of cinch straps on the sides and at the waist so that it can be tightened to fit like a pair of shoes--snug but comfortable. If it's not worn properly, or doesn't fit

A simple fitting test for a PFD involves pulling up on its shoulders.
The PFD should stay in place around your body.

correctly, a PFD can actually impede your ability to swim rather than help. A good fit test that you can do on dry land is to put on the PFD and tighten it as you would to wear it on the water. Hooking your thumbs under the shoulder straps and hauling upward, your PFD should stay in place around your body and not ride up around your ears.

Any PFD that is Coast Guard Approved, fits well, and is comfortable enough so that you won't feel the need to remove it while on the water, is perfectly adequate. With that said, the best PFDs for kayaking are the ones specifically designed for that purpose. Kayaking PFDs feature large armholes, and the bulk of their flotation is moved down away from the shoulders and upper chest to allow the fullest range of arm and upper body motion for maximum comfort while paddling. Many PFDs also have convenient features such as zippered pockets for carrying such things as sunscreen, glasses, and snacks. Some models even have pouches for hydration bladders that can be mounted on the back of the PFD.

DRESSING TO GO KAYAKING

In hot temperatures and warm water, dressing for kayaking is a snap. The biggest challenge you'll likely face is staying cool, hydrated, and protected from the sun. Sunscreen is an absolute necessity, as is a hat to shade your head and neck. Sunglasses are also a real asset, especially when paddling in the morning or late afternoon when the sun is low and its glare off the water is blinding. Just remember to wear some type of retainer strap so that you don't lose them overboard. The best way to protect your skin from the harmful rays of the sun is simply to cover it. For this reason, I often opt to paddle in a long-sleeved shirt even on warm, sunny days. Below the waist, fast-drying nylon shorts and a pair of sandals work well.

Dressing for cold water is far more difficult, especially when the air is warm. Even on the hottest days, if the water is frigid, immersion can quickly lead to hypothermia. Choosing the right clothes is challenging, because while cold water will quickly drain the warmth from your body, wearing the clothing necessary to keep you warm in

Sun protection is always important on the water, where the glare can be blinding at times.

A Farmer John wetsuit is great, affordable insurance against cold water.

A dry suit is the ultimate in protection against the cold.

the event of an unplanned swim can result in serious overheating when you're not immersed. A neoprene wetsuit is one of the best options for these conditions. A neoprene Farmer John provides good insulation for a modest price, and the cut of the garment allows a full range of movement in the shoulder without chafing. A wetsuit is a great foundation piece for your paddling wardrobe because as temperatures drop, you can add more clothing for more warmth.

When both the water and the air temperature are cold, hypothermia is obviously a serious concern. In these conditions, bundle up, and be sure to select fabrics that insulate well even when wet. Synthetic fabrics like polyester fleece, polypropylene, and neoprene are excellent because they retain a good degree of their insulating value when wet. Wool is also a fine insulator, but is slow to dry and heavy when wet. Avoid cotton at all cost, as it's one of the all-time worst materials to wear around cold water. Not only does it dry really slowly, but it actually draws heat away from your body--which does make it a good choice for really hot weather. You'll also want to have an outer shell that keeps the wind off your body. A waterproof nylon jacket and pants do just this. For your feet, neoprene booties and a pair of wool socks will keep your tootsies warm. The ultimate protection against the cold is a dry suit. A dry suit uses latex gaskets at the ankles, wrists and neck to keep all water out, even when you're completely immersed. Dry suits are expensive, but if you spend a lot of time paddling in cold conditions it will be a great investment in both comfort and safety.

Of course, the best strategy of all is to avoid capsizing altogether, and by paddling in protected areas and playing conservatively, you will be highly unlikely to ever capsize your boat. Recreational kayaks are so stable that as long as you're paddling in a sheltered area that isn't subject to strong wind or waves, there's no reason to flip. As an added precaution, it's also important that you stay close to shore, so that in the event of a capsize, you can quickly swim to safety while your paddling buddies gather your equipment. The type of boat that you're paddling will also dictate how you'll need to dress in cold water. If you're paddling a sit-on-top kayak, you should expect your lower body to be very wet, whereas a sit-inside will provide far more protection from the elements.

There are a number of other pieces of clothing that come in handy, and most kayaks have plenty of room to bring extra gear along. A wooly hat is a great addition on a chilly day as are paddling gloves. If you're using a sit-inside kayak, you can also wear a sprayskirt. On chilly days or in frigid water, a sprayskirt will keep cold water out of the boat and allow your body heat to warm up the interior of the cockpit. On hot days, a sprayskirt will shade your legs from the sun.

SAFETY EQUIPMENT

Kayaking is inherently very safe. With a conservative attitude and a liberal application of good old-fashioned common sense, you can avoid virtually all hazardous situations, but you still need to be prepared for the worst. Sometimes unforeseen complications overtake even the most safety-conscious paddlers. The safety gear that should accompany you on the water will vary depending on the type of outing you're undertaking. By staying close to shore and only paddling on sheltered, easily accessed

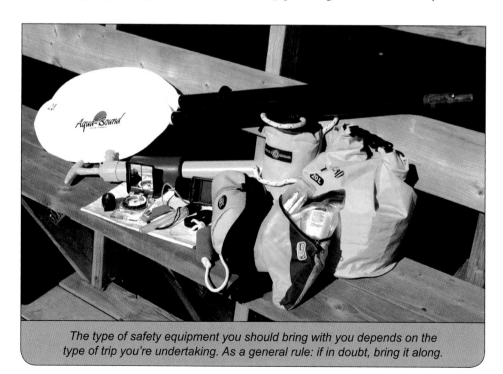

The type of safety equipment you should bring with you depends on the type of trip you're undertaking. As a general rule: if in doubt, bring it along.

waterways where you don't need to worry about wind, waves, current, or having to spend an unplanned night out in the wilderness, you will need very little in the way of rescue equipment. In these settings, your best piece of safety equipment is your PFD, so make sure you're wearing it at all times. It's also a good idea to always bring a whistle, water, and a snack. Although most people wouldn't consider all these things "safety gear," keeping your energy level high is an important factor in staying safe and happy.

As soon as you stray into more exposed conditions, you will suddenly need to include far more safety equipment, along with the training and practice to use it effectively. If you plan on paddling farther from shore than you can comfortably swim, or decide to venture along rugged shorelines that don't provide escape from the water, or if you long to paddle in waves, wind, or current, then you really need to take a course. You'll learn about how to avoid rescue situations in the first place, as well as how to use the various pieces of safety equipment that can let you deal with the situations that can arise all too quickly on unprotected waters.

CHECKLIST

It's my hope that this checklist will help you avoid the awkward moments I've experienced when I show up at the put-in without a key piece of gear. Having learned my lesson numerous times (and more and more often as I've gotten older), I now use a big Rubbermaid™ container to transport my paddling gear in the back of my vehicle—a cheap and waterproof solution. On the lid of the container, I've taped a laminated copy of this checklist so I can just mentally tick off items as I toss them in. Be sure to customize your personal list so that it reflects the paddling conditions that you face and the items that you need to bring along. Now if I could only find my car keys . . .

Paddling Gear Checklist

- ☐ Kayak
- ☐ Paddle and paddle leash
- ☐ PFD
- ☐ Sprayskirt
- ☐ Sponge
- ☐ Surf shorts
- ☐ Paddling shirt
- ☐ Windbreaker
- ☐ Sandals
- ☐ Hat
- ☐ Sunglasses and strap
- ☐ Sun block
- ☐ Water bottle and energy bar

Other

- ☐ Waterproof camera
- ☐ Super Soaker water cannon
- ☐ Dry bag with fleece shirt and pants
- ☐ Fishing rod and tackle
- ☐ Wetsuit

CHAPTER TWO

BEFORE HITTING THE WATER

CARING FOR A KAYAK • TRANSPORTING YOUR KAYAK
CARRYING YOUR KAYAK • GETTING IN AND OUT OF YOUR KAYAK
SITTING IN A KAYAK • USING YOUR PADDLE

CARING FOR A KAYAK

Kayaks are pretty simple machines and don't require a whole lot of maintenance, but there are a few things that you can do to prolong their life and keep them looking good. For instance, salt is amazingly corrosive, so it's great if you can rinse your kayak with fresh water after it's been in salt water. Pay special attention to rinsing any moving or metal parts like rudders or adjustable pedals.

Another way to keep your boat looking its best is to store it properly. One of the best things you can do for your kayak is to store it out of the sun. Over time, exposure to the sun will make the plastic more brittle. Ideally, your kayak should be stored in a cool, dry place, like a garage. If you're storing it outside, try to keep it in a shaded area or at least out of the sun when it's at its highest and most powerful. You should also roll the kayak onto its side or completely upside down to make sure rainwater can't drain into the boat. Water weighs a LOT, and can easily warp or seriously damage your kayak if it's left inside for any length of time. Pools of stagnant water will also provide a great breeding ground for green slime, mosquitoes, and other creepy crawlies.

DINGS, DENTS AND DAMAGE . . . OH MY!

One of the greatest things about plastic boats is their durability. They can withstand amazing impacts, scrapes, and general abuse, but they will show their battle scars. Scratches in the bottom of your boat are nothing to worry about, unless they are so deep that they virtually go right through the hull. I like to think of each scratch as an individual record of all the good times I've had in my kayak. If you do want to clean up the bottom of your boat, your best bet is to use a razor blade to remove any strings of plastic that may be hanging off.

One of the few downsides of plastic boats is their tendency to deform over time. The most common deformation is the warping of the hull, which is commonly referred to as "oil canning." Oil canning is often a result of prolonged exposure to the sun, or of being stored in the same position for long periods of time. You'll even get oil canning from cinching your boat down on your roof racks. It's important to know that unless the deformity is severe, it really doesn't affect the boat's performance, and shouldn't be a cause for concern. If the boat is showing serious warping or dents, heat will often be enough to return the kayak to its original shape. On a hot day, leaving your kayak in the sun can be enough to pop out dents. If that doesn't work, you can dump some hot water into the kayak and use your hands (don't burn yourself!) to encourage some of the dents out.

With enough force, it's possible to crack or puncture a kayak, which is a serious problem that will definitely require full repair before going out on the water again. This type of damage is most common with composite kayaks, and can be repaired relatively easily by someone experienced in fiberglass work.

TRANSPORTING YOUR KAYAK

It doesn't take a rocket scientist to realize that strapping a kayak to the roof of a car can be a real recipe for disaster. In fact, most serious damage to kayaks is incurred during transportation, not while in use on the water.

Most important, and often dismissed, is the need for a good and solidly attached set of roof racks. Unfortunately, factory-installed roof racks are seldom ideal. After-market racks from manufacturers like Yakima or Thule are the ultimate solution for hauling kayaks. They have racks to fit virtually any vehicle, as well as unique systems such as kayak rollers and cradles that do a great job of protecting your boat and make loading and tying the kayaks safer and easier. If you are using simple (but strong) bar racks, it's a good idea to pad the racks with foam to save your kayak some scratches and wear.

Although loading a kayak onto the roof of a vehicle can be done by one strong person, it is much easier with two people--one at each end. The simplest solution for

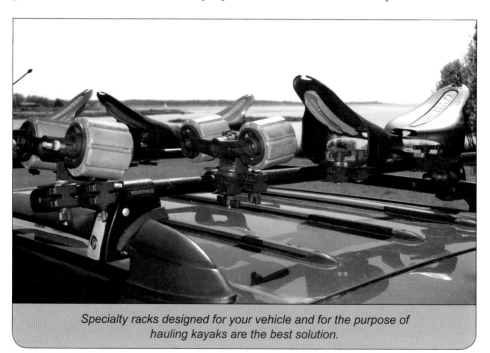

Specialty racks designed for your vehicle and for the purpose of hauling kayaks are the best solution.

loading a kayak is to invest in some kayak rollers. You can then lift one end up onto the rollers and push the kayak all the way on to the vehicle from behind.

To tie your boat down, ropes work well enough, but cam straps are quicker and more reliable. Regardless of which you use, securely tying a boat onto your roof racks is pretty easy. As long as you don't strap it down at its widest point, your kayak will resist flying off. Don't be afraid to aggressively tighten straps when securing plastic boats. The chances of hurting them are slim. With fiberglass or thermoformed kayaks, a much more delicate touch is needed.

Sit-inside kayaks are easy to tie on securely. As long as you have a strap on each side of the cockpit, the coaming will help prevent the boat from sliding forward or backward. Something to keep in mind about sit-inside kayaks is that if they are left upright on your vehicle overnight, they can collect a surprising amount of rainwater. This will make them much heavier, and it will likely be best to drain boats before driving anywhere. Be careful when unloading boats containing water--not only are they very heavy, you may also get soaked wrestling them off the roof. An added piece of insurance for a secure boat is to tie a bowline or stern line to your kayak, although you don't want to tie them too tightly, as that will bend your boat along its length.

On a final note, expect your tie job to loosen after driving for a while, especially on rough backcountry roads or in wet conditions. Losing a kayak off the roof of your car is no laughing matter and can end in disaster, so take the time and pull over to double check that your kayak is secure.

The most secure tie-down involves two straps around
the middle of the kayak, along with a bowline and sternline.

CARRYING YOUR KAYAK

The majority of recreational kayaks are made out of polyethylene plastic--an incredibly durable and affordable material. One of the downsides to plastic is that it makes for a fairly heavy kayak. Plastic kayaks range from thirty to seventy pounds, with most weighing in at around fifty pounds. Composite kayaks are about 15% lighter, and thermoformed kayaks fall somewhere in between.

The great thing about plastic kayaks is that if you need to, you can get away with dragging your boat to the water, while doing this to a composite or thermoformed boat isn't really an option. Of course, dragging your plastic kayak will give it a very used look quite quickly and can eventually wear it out, although it would take a LOT of dragging. Quite often, though, it's just the easiest way to get where you're going and it's nice to have that option.

The next easiest means of carrying a kayak is with a two-person tandem carry, where each person grabs the handle at either end of the boat. Many hands DO make light work, so you should never hesitate to ask for a helping hand. On the same note, you'll get more help if you take the initiative and offer your assistance to others.

An option for really strong people is a solo shoulder carry. This can work well for sit-in kayaks, as the cockpit coaming will sit nicely on your shoulder. The challenge is

*Many hands make light work and the tandem carry
is the easiest way to carry kayaks.*

To lift a kayak solo, start by pulling the boat up to your thighs.

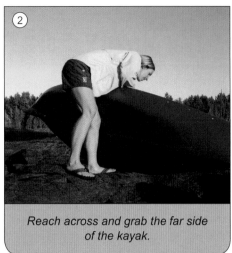

Reach across and grab the far side of the kayak.

Using your knee to help lift, roll the kayak up to your shoulder.

With the cockpit coaming resting on your shoulder, you are ready to go.

usually in getting the kayak onto your shoulder in the first place. When doing so, make sure you bend your legs and keep your back as straight as possible. Start by lifting the boat onto your thighs, cockpit out. Next, grasp the far edge of the coaming, and then roll the boat up and onto your shoulder. To put the kayak back down, simply reverse the steps.

Another great option is a kayak cart. Kayak carts are basically cradles with two wheels that support one end of the kayak, while you pull the boat along from the other end. Most carts pack down to store inside, or on top of the deck of a kayak.

GETTING IN AND OUT OF YOUR KAYAK

Getting into a kayak is easy in most cases. The only real rule to follow is to "get your butt into the boat quickly." With your butt in the seat, your center of gravity will be low and you'll feel nice and stable. It's only the awkward transition between standing and sitting where trouble usually occurs.

The easiest spots to get into and out of your kayak are beaches. On a nice sandy beach, you can hop into your boat with it resting at the edge of the water, and then just push yourself out with your hands when you're ready. You can also get into your

When getting in from a dock, start from a sitting position with your feet in the boat.

Turn towards the bow and place both hands firmly on the dock.

Sit down as quickly as possible into the seat.

Once settled, grab your paddle and push away from the dock.

boat while it floats in a few inches of water. Simply straddle your floating kayak, with a foot on either side of it, and drop your butt quickly into the seat to sit down. Then pull your legs in after you. This entry technique is a better method for getting into your boat if you've got a composite or thermoform kayak that you don't want to scuff along the sand. Unfortunately, it's a lot less effective if there are any waves rolling into the beach. Even small waves can bat your kayak around easily. If you have waves to contend with, you're best off getting into your kayak on shore and then pushing yourself out.

If your launch site requires that you get into your boat from a dock, choose the dock's lowest point for the task. The higher the dock, the more difficult getting in will be. Start by positioning your kayak parallel to the dock, and then sit down on the dock beside the kayak's seat. Place your paddle close by, so that it will be within easy reach once you are in your boat. Next, put your feet in the kayak close to the centerline of the boat, for maximum stability. Now turn your body towards the bow of the kayak, securing a good grip with both hands on the dock, and then lower yourself decisively into the seat. To get out, you can simply reverse these steps.

For awkward or rocky launch sites, the best way to get into your boat involves floating your kayak in the water, and then using your paddle as an outrigger for support. Place your paddle at ninety degrees to the kayak with the shaft resting on the boat just behind the cockpit, and the far blade supported on shore. Grasp the paddle shaft and coaming behind your back, and squat down beside the kayak. Cheating your

When getting in or out of your kayak on a rocky shoreline,
you can use your paddle as an outrigger for support.

weight onto the outrigger, slip your legs into the boat and drop your butt into the seat. You can get out of your kayak on uneven or rocky shorelines using this same technique in reverse, although it will be difficult if you have any waves to contend with.

SITTING IN A KAYAK

Kayak outfitting has become more and more comfortable. So comfortable, in fact, that it sometimes promotes lounging rather than good paddling posture. Although there's certainly nothing wrong with a little lounging, and while I may be somewhat partial to it myself, we're going to take a quick look at the ideal sitting position for paddling a kayak. Maintaining good posture in a boat will allow you to paddle more comfortably, promote more efficient strokes, and help avoid issues like back pain.

The ideal sitting position in a kayak is comfortably upright. Just like your mom always told you to sit at the dinner table! Your feet should be resting comfortably and securely against the foot pedals or in the foot wells. Your legs should be comfortably flexed and somewhat splayed out. Keeping your knees slightly bent will make sitting upright easier and reduce the strain on your hamstrings and back. Most kayaks now come with some type of back support. A seatback or back band not only helps turn your kayak into a great lounge chair, when tightened they also encourage an upright sitting position.

Although there's nothing wrong with lounging in your kayak, when paddling you should sit upright.

One of the most common reasons for discomfort in a kayak is tight hamstrings. Tight hamstrings make it difficult to sit up straight with your legs out in front of you. If you're experiencing discomfort while paddling, take the time to do some regular stretching. It doesn't take long, and will quickly improve your flexibility and increase your comfort in a kayak.

USING YOUR PADDLE

The paddle is such an important component for every kayaker because it provides the most direct contact with the water. It translates a paddler's energy into input for accelerating forward, changing direction, stopping, or turning. We've already discussed how to choose a paddle, so now let's look at how to use it.

To start off, if you are paddling "feathered" (with the two blades of your paddle at different angles), you need to decide which your control hand is. In general, if you are right-handed, your right hand will be your control hand. Likewise the left hand will be control hand for left-handed paddlers. This "control" hand keeps a firm grip on the shaft at all times, which is why it is also referred to as the "glue" hand. The control hand's grip should never change, whether you're forward paddling, back paddling, or

A secure, but light grip on the paddle will make paddling more comfortable and help you avoid overuse injuiries such as tendonitis in the wrist.

performing any other stroke. The knuckles of your control hand should be aligned along the same plane as that side's paddle blade. After taking a stroke with the blade by your control hand, you'll loosen your grip with the opposite hand, which is often referred to as the "grease" hand, so that you can rotate the shaft within it. This rotation is necessary to accommodate the "feather," or "twist," of your paddle, and lets you place the next blade in the water squarely. This loosening of the "grease" hand, and the rotation of the shaft within it, takes place between each stroke.

If you're using a paddle with no feather/twist, you won't need to worry about rotating the shaft between strokes. Many people find this more intuitive and natural than a feathered paddle stroke. Try it both ways and go with what feels most comfortable for you.

Your grip on the paddle shaft will also have a big impact on how effective your strokes are. Your grip on the paddle should be secure but light, with your hands equal distances from the blades. A light grip will let you paddle more comfortably for longer, and will help you avoid overuse injuries such as tendonitis in the wrist.

To figure out how far your hands should be apart, and to establish the best hand position on the shaft, try lifting your paddle up onto your head. Once your arms are bent at an angle of approximately ninety degrees, your grip will be about right. This hand placement gives you the best mix of control and power.

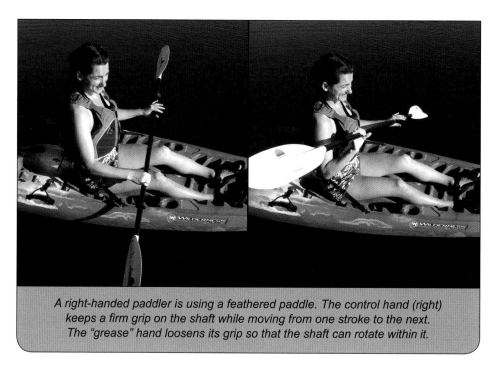

A right-handed paddler is using a feathered paddle. The control hand (right) keeps a firm grip on the shaft while moving from one stroke to the next. The "grease" hand loosens its grip so that the shaft can rotate within it.

PADDLE FACT

The ocean provides the most dramatic natural playgrounds for paddlers, although extra care needs to be taken when paddling in these types of environments.

CHAPTER THREE

THE ESSENTIAL STROKES & TECHNIQUES

FORWARD STROKE • REVERSE STROKE • SWEEP STROKE
DRAW STROKE •   PADDLING TANDEM KAYAKS
GETTING BACK INTO YOUR KAYAK FROM THE WATER

While kayaking is generally very intuitive, there are some "key strokes" that are truly worth taking the time to learn properly. With the addition of these strokes to your paddling repertoire, you'll be able to travel on the water efficiently and maneuver very effectively. Good boat control will provide a dramatic boost in confidence, letting you get even more enjoyment from your time on the water, and it will open the doors to new, more advanced skills and maneuvers, should you choose to pursue them.

FORWARD STROKE

The forward stroke is the most important stroke, for obvious reasons--it is essential that you be able to travel across the water smoothly and efficiently. Although any stroke that gets your kayak moving forward is fine, by learning correct technique you'll be able to get where you want to go more efficiently and with the least amount of wasted effort. Good technique will also promote a high level of comfort on the water and go a long way to eliminating the pain associated with overstressed muscles and joints.

The forward stroke can be broken down into three parts: the catch, rotation, and recovery.

THE CATCH

The catch is the all-important start to the forward stroke, where your paddle blade is planted in the water. Sitting up straight, with a relaxed grip on your paddle, reach to your toes and plant your blade fully into the water. This reaching action involves both your arms and your shoulders. Do not lean forward at the waist to reach to your toes, but rather twist from the waist. If you're reaching for a stroke with your right blade, you'll push your right shoulder forward while reaching with your right arm. This shoulder-reach causes you to rotate or "wind-up" your upper torso, and is commonly referred to as torso rotation. Torso rotation lets you harness the power of your front and side stomach muscles for your strokes, rather than just using your arms. With your body wound up, spear your blade into the water so that the whole blade is submerged. Once that blade is completely in the water, you'll then pull on your paddle and unwind your upper body to drive your boat forward.

One of the most common mistakes is pulling on the forward stroke before the blade is fully planted in the water. If you're doing this, you'll notice your strokes creating a lot of splash, which means that you're actually wasting energy pulling water past your kayak, rather than pulling your kayak forward through the water. To understand this better, imagine that you're planting your paddle in cement when you take a stroke. The paddle shouldn't really move anywhere once it's planted. Instead, you're pulling yourself past that paddle. The only way this will work is if you have fully and securely planted your whole blade in the water.

ROTATION

Once it's wound up, your body is like a powerful spring, putting a lot of potential energy at your command. Rotation refers to the way you'll use this energy to power your forward stroke.

As described above, after the catch, your body should be wound up and your paddle firmly planted at your toes. You'll now pull on your paddle and drive your kayak forward using as much of your large torso muscles as possible, rather than relying on your comparatively weak arms to do the work. In fact, a good way to think about this is that your arms are just a supplement to the power of your torso. True power comes from your stomach, side, and back muscles. (If you don't believe it, try paddling forward with your arms locked straight at the elbows.) It may not be comfortable to paddle like this, but you can really get your boat moving, and the only way to do it is with pronounced rotation.

Now that you're engaging the most powerful muscles, let's take a quick look at what the rest of your body will be doing. With elbows bent and staying low, pull on the paddle with your arms as you take each stroke. The range of motion of your arms is actually quite

To plant your forward stroke, reach to your toes by twisting at the waist.

Make sure that as you pull on your stroke, the blade is fully submerged.

The forward stroke ends and your paddle is sliced up out of the water once it reaches your hip.

Photo by: thilobrunner.com

small, since your torso will be doing the bulk of the work. As a general rule, the more vertical the paddle shaft is while taking a forward stroke, the more power you're getting from it. To get the paddle more vertical, bring your top hand higher and further across your boat. These sprinting strokes are great when you're in a hurry, but they're also very tiring. For general paddling purposes, keep your top hand about shoulder or chest level.

For maximum drive, your legs can also be involved with your forward stroke. By pushing with the foot on the same side that you're taking a stroke on, you will help transfer more power to your stroke.

RECOVERY

The recovery is the point at which your forward stroke ends and the blade gets removed from the water. This happens at your hip, which is earlier than most paddlers expect or practice. When your stroke reaches your hip, slice your paddle up out of the water sideways and get ready for the next stroke. At this point, your body should have unwound past its position of rest, and be wound up ready for the next catch of your other blade on the opposite side. So spear your blade deeply into the water, and then pull the next stroke through.

Now that you have all the pieces for an efficient and powerful forward stroke, try to put them all together as smoothly as possible while keeping your boat as quiet as you can. A "quiet" boat has minimal bob from side to side or up and down, and will glide through the water most efficiently.

REVERSE STROKE

Although you might not use the reverse stroke very often, it can come in very handy when maneuvering in confined spaces, and is definitely worth learning.

The reverse stroke is just like the forward stroke, only done in reverse. However, this does not mean that you spin the paddle in your hands when performing the stroke. Instead, your grip on the shaft remains the same as always, and the back face of the paddle is used to push water.

The reverse stroke starts just behind your hip and ends at your toes. Your top hand is held in a relaxed position in front of your body between chest and chin height. As you plant your blade deeply in the water behind your hip, turn your upper body in that same direction. With your body rotated towards your paddle, you can use the power of torso rotation to help your stroke by unwinding your body as you push your blade towards the bow. As your stroke reaches your toes, your body should be wound up in the other direction and ready for the next stroke on the opposite side.

As a final note, when reversing, always remember to be sure and keep an eye on where you're going, or you're sure to collide with something or someone. I like to look over my shoulder every few strokes and it's easiest to do this by turning my head to the same side as my stroke, taking a quick glance over that shoulder just as I plant my blade in the water.

The reverse stroke uses the backside of your paddle, starts just behind your hip, and ends at your toes. Make sure you keep on eye on where you're going.

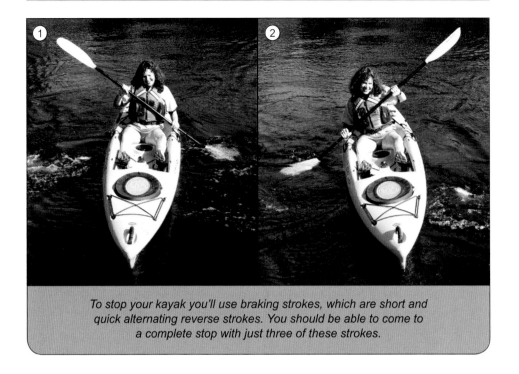

To stop your kayak you'll use braking strokes, which are short and quick alternating reverse strokes. You should be able to come to a complete stop with just three of these strokes.

SWEEP STROKE

Most recreational kayaks are designed to travel well in a straight line, which means that you can't expect them to turn on a dime. When you do need to turn them, you'll use sweep strokes. There are both forward and reverse sweep strokes, and both can be used while stationary or moving.

FORWARD SWEEP

The forward sweep stroke is a great way to turn your kayak while stationary or moving. It's a truly excellent stroke for making course corrections while traveling forward, because it allows you turn your boat while keeping your speed going, rather than killing all your forward momentum.

Just like the forward stroke, the forward sweep starts with your body wound up, and your blade completely in the water at your toes. It also harnesses the power of torso rotation. Unlike the forward propelling stroke, your hands will stay very low during the sweep and your blade will follow an arcing path as far out to the side of your kayak as possible. To do this, the hand controlling the active blade will reach out over the water, while the other maintains a low position in front of your

The forward sweep is planted at the toes with the paddle kept low to the water.

Make sure the blade is planted firmly on the water and sweep a wide arc out to the side of your kayak.

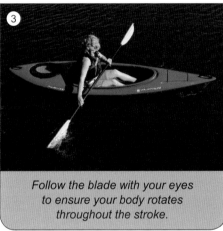

Follow the blade with your eyes to ensure your body rotates throughout the stroke.

Slice your paddle out of the water before it touches the stern.

stomach. Your blade will continue on its arcing path until it approaches the stern of your boat. You'll then slice your paddle out of the water before it touches the stern, and move to your next stroke.

To get the most power from your torso rotation, sit upright in your kayak and watch your active blade throughout its arc. Following the blade with your eyes will force your upper body to rotate throughout the stroke. You can also push off the foot pedal on the sweeping-stroke side of the boat for even more power.

REVERSE SWEEP

The reverse sweep is exactly what it sounds like--a forward sweep stroke done in reverse, and like the back stroke, you'll use the back face of your paddle. The reverse sweep can be used while stationary, or when traveling forward, although it's important to note

The reverse sweep starts at the stern of your kayak, with your eyes and body turned to face the active blade.

With your paddle planted firmly in the water, sweep a wide arc out to the side of your kayak.

Keep that paddle blade in the water.

Finish the stroke before your paddle hits the side of your kayak.

that it will kill almost all of your speed, which can be helpful when you need to put on the brakes and make a major course correction.

The reverse sweep begins with your body wound up and your blade completely in the water at the stern of your kayak, about six inches away from the hull. In order to get the most torso rotation possible into your stroke, keep your eyes on your active paddle blade. With your blade planted deeply in the water, sweep a wide arc all the way out to the side of your kayak, up to your toes. The hand controlling the active blade reaches out over the water, while the other takes up position in front of your stomach. Track the progress of your blade by watching it throughout its arc. By keeping your head turning with your active blade, you will encourage good torso rotation and ensure that your body unwinds throughout the whole stroke.

Once you're comfortable with both the forward and reverse sweeps, try combining a forward sweep on one side, with a reverse sweep on the opposite side. You'll find that this combination of strokes is so effective that you can virtually spin your kayak in place.

DRAW STROKE

Draw strokes are used to move your kayak sideways. The draw is an amazingly useful maneuvering stroke for pulling yourself up beside a dock, or whenever you want to close the distance between yourself and another paddler.

The basic draw involves reaching out to the side of your hip, planting your blade, and then pulling your boat and body sideways toward it. For the most effective stroke, plant your blade completely in the water, rotate your head and upper body to face your active blade, and get your paddle shaft as vertical as possible. Getting your paddle shaft vertical will require reaching across your upper body with your top hand, which takes good balance, so you might want to start by practicing your draw stroke with your top hand in front of your face. When your blade is completely in the water, pull your lower hand in towards your hip. Your top hand will stay very stationary, acting as the pivot point for the stroke. Before your paddle hits your boat, you'll need to finish the stroke by slicing the blade out of the water towards the stern. Be careful that you do not bring your paddle too close to the side of your kayak before finishing the stroke. The paddle should exit about six inches away from the side. If you do pin the paddle up against your kayak, it can easily lever your boat upside down, flipping you with surprising speed!

One of the most common problems people have with the draw stroke is that they find that it turns their kayak rather than moving it only sideways. If you experience this problem, it generally means that you're pulling your draw too far forward or too far back. If you're pulling your draw too far forward (towards your knee instead of your hip) you'll pull your bow towards your paddle. If your draw is too far back, you'll

The draw stroke is a great way to pull up alongside a dock.
The draw stroke involves reaching out to the side of the kayak and then
pulling in towards your hip using the power face of your paddle.

pull your stern towards your paddle. Drawing your paddle towards your hip is a good guideline, but every kayak reacts differently and you can expect to need to make some fine adjustments to keep your boat moving perfectly sideways.

PADDLING TANDEM KAYAKS

Tandem kayaks or "doubles" are a great way for two people--who may have very different paddling experience or skill sets--to get out on the water and share the joy of kayaking together. Typically wider than single kayaks, tandems have awesome stability, which makes them ideal platforms for introducing to the sport of kayaking those who may be a little nervous about being out on the water. You can take almost anyone kayaking in a tandem, whether it's your kids, your parents, your grandparents, or even your dog. A great thing about tandems is that your passengers don't even need to paddle if they don't want to. Just sit them in the bow and take them on a tour of the bay!

Although tandems provide a great opportunity for taking a passenger for a ride, if both people are paddling, tandems can travel surprisingly quickly. The most efficient way of paddling a tandem is for both occupants to paddle in unison. Not only will this drive the kayak forward the quickest, you'll also avoid the clashing of paddles. If there is one paddler who is physically stronger than the other, the weaker paddler traditionally sits in the bow and dictates the paddling pace. The "motor" sits in the back of the boat and modifies his or her stroke rate to keep the bow paddler's pace.

You can take almost anyone out on the water in a tandem kayak.

The best way to turn a tandem kayak has the front paddler taking a forward sweep on one side, and the back paddler taking a reverse sweep on the other side.

Something to keep in mind is that the size of your paddle blades is like the size of chain rings on a bike, so if there is a weaker paddler, he or she should ideally be using smaller blades in order to keep a similar paddling pace to the stronger paddler. It is also preferable (although not crucial) to use slightly longer paddles for a tandem than you would for a single kayak, because of the boat's added width.

Some tandems are equipped with a rudder, which aids greatly in maneuvering the kayak and making small course corrections. The best way to turn a tandem kayak while stationary involves a little teamwork. Ideally, the front paddler takes a forward sweep on one side, while the stern paddler performs a reverse sweep on the opposite side of the kayak.

If you think that tandem kayaks won't be as much fun as singles, think again. In fact, sit-on-top tandem kayaks are so stable that you could consider them to be high-performance floating docks, which makes them terrific for families. Watching kids play with a tandem kayak at the lake, you'll see the boat transform in seconds from a pirate ship, to an aircraft carrier, to a diving platform. Tandem kayaks can be so many different things to different people, and this is what makes them one of the most versatile and fun watercrafts from the cottage to the coast.

GETTING BACK INTO YOUR KAYAK FROM THE WATER

One of the huge advantages of sit-on-top kayaks is the fact that they are so easy to get back into from the water. This means that they make great swimming platforms in addition to fulfilling the more standard kayak functions. Sit-inside kayaks are more difficult to get back into from the water, but with a little practice and some help from a friend, you can learn to quickly and reliably re-enter a sit-inside, too. Something to remember, though, is that since sit-insides aren't self-bailing you'll have a lot of water to pump out of your kayak once you're back in the seat.

RE-ENTERING A SIT-ON-TOP FROM THE WATER

Start by positioning yourself alongside the kayak, by the seat. You can keep your paddle in one hand, slide it under your deck lines so that it doesn't get away from you, or give it to your paddling buddy. With a firm grip on the kayak, let your legs float to the surface behind you. You'll then give a powerful kick with your legs and push with your arms to haul your chest up onto the kayak. Once you're up on the boat, twist

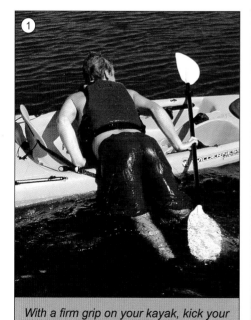

With a firm grip on your kayak, kick your legs and pull your chest onto the kayak.

You'll then twist your body and settle into the seat.

your body around and settle into the seat. You can then swing your legs back onto the boat to complete the re-entry. Mission accomplished.

RE-ENTERING A SIT-INSIDE FROM THE WATER

As already mentioned, re-entering a sit-inside kayak from the water is more complicated. It's also more difficult, as the deck of a sit-inside kayak is higher above the water surface, which means that you'll have a harder time climbing up on it. This also means that you will be less stable once you're up there. Although it is possible to re-enter a sit-inside on your own, it is a technique that takes training and practice, and is not something we're going to look at in this book. Instead, we're going to explore a technique for re-entering a sit-inside kayak with the help of another paddler.

The first order of business is to flip your boat upright if it's upside down. When your boat is upside down, air is trapped inside, which is keeping water from flooding the interior. This means that the quicker you can flip the boat upright, the less water will get scooped inside. Although you can flip the kayak upright yourself from the water, your paddling buddy can help by lifting an end as you roll the kayak. With the kayak upright, your paddling partner can stabilize the kayak as you get back in. A partner can actually provide an incredible amount of stability, although it requires a lot of commitment on his or her part. Positioning the kayak parallel to yours and getting a good grip on the empty kayak with both hands, the partner then leans his/her whole body over onto it. As long as he has a good grip on the kayak, there's virtually no chance of his flipping himself, as the two "rafted" kayaks will be extremely stable. You can then use virtually the same re-entry technique as the one outlined for the sit-on-top kayak.

Position yourself alongside the kayak just behind the seat and grab the cockpit rim,

Once your boat is upright, another paddler will stabilize your kayak by getting a firm grip on it and leaning his/her body over onto it.

With a kick of your legs and push with your arms, pull your chest onto the stern deck.

Lying chest down, turn towards the stern, slide your legs in the boat, and then corkscrew back into the seat.

The helping paddler should keep the boat stable until you're ready to go again.

which provides a nice handle. Let your legs float to the surface behind you and then with a powerful kick and push of the arms, haul your chest up and onto the stern deck. Lying chest down, turn your head towards the stern and slide your legs into the cockpit. You'll then twist your body to corkscrew settle your butt back into the seat and then pull your legs back into the boat, and you're ready to go. Of course, you will have a fair amount of water in the boat to deal with after re-entry. This is why sea and touring kayakers carry a bilge pump, a device specifically designed to pump water from a boat without going to shore. Although a bilge pump is a great piece of safety gear for any sit-inside kayak, you should also make a practice of always paddling close enough to shore so that you can easily head to dry land and empty your boat there.

PADDLE FACT

Some Hobie Kayaks have foot pedal systems that drive the kayak forward.

CHAPTER FOUR

ON WATER SAFETY

Photo courtesy of Innova Kayaks

CHOOSING A GOOD PADDLING LOCATION • DEALING WITH WEATHER
ON WATER TRAFFIC • SEA HAZARDS • RIVER HAZARDS

You'll be happy to hear that kayaking is a remarkably safe and user-friendly activity. In fact, compared to most other outdoor activities, the chances of getting hurt while kayaking are very small. With that said, it is important to understand that when things do go wrong when kayaking, the fact that you're on the water means that situations can become very serious, very quickly. It's for this reason that it is important that you understand and appreciate the risks and hazards involved with kayaking, and that you assume a conservative and safety-conscious attitude when making decisions on the water.

Research has shown that there are five factors that are common elements of boating accidents.

Avoiding dangerous situations on the water is surprisingly easy. First and foremost, understand that alcohol and boating simply don't go together. Regrettably, alcohol is a major factor in all boating accidents. It's also critical that you wear a PFD whenever you're on the water. By investing in a kayaking-specific PFD that is designed to be as comfortable and unrestricting as possible while seated and paddling in a kayak, you'll eliminate virtually any reason for wanting to remove it. On a similar note, you need to dress for the conditions. Cold water represents the biggest hazard, as being immersed in cold water can result in hypothermia very quickly. If you're paddling in cold water, you need to be more conservative with all your decisions. Paddle only in calm conditions, stay close to shore, never paddle alone, and keep in mind that you're better off overdressing and being too warm than being too cold. With all that cold water around, it's easy to cool yourself off!

Photo by theboulter.com

CHOOSING A GOOD PADDLING LOCATION

One of the easiest ways to stay safe and ensure that your paddling experience is fun for everyone is to choose an appropriate paddling location. One of the greatest things about kayaking is that there are so many great spots to explore, whether you live near a lake, river, pond, or the ocean. Most importantly, you'll want to pick a location that is very sheltered from both wind and waves. Although the ocean and large lakes can sometimes be incredibly calm, providing an ideal kayaking environment, you do need to appreciate how quickly weather can turn. This means that if you plan on paddling in exposed areas, where conditions can deteriorate really quickly, it's important that you always check the weather forecast before heading out, and that you keep your eyes open for signs of bad weather moving in. Also make sure that you know of a variety of different take-out points, so that you won't feel compelled to challenge the elements in order to get back to the one place you know to get out.

The ideal kayaking environment has a good access point for launching, lots of places to easily go ashore, and minimal motorized on-water traffic. Seek out calm bays, or quiet lakes and river ways. And hey, if there just happens to be a hotdog stand or a little shack that sells the world's best fish tacos nearby, that's just fine! Although it can

The ideal boat launch is a sheltered beach without waves.

be tempting to search out the most remote location possible, bear in mind that if you ever did need a little assistance, it's awfully nice to know that there will be someone around who can lend a hand. By the same token, that's why it's not a great idea to paddle alone. There really is safety in numbers when it comes to being out on the water, so always paddle with a group, or at least another buddy who can come to your aid (or vice versa) should an unforeseen situation arise.

DEALING WITH WEATHER

Weather obviously has a huge bearing on when and where you should go kayaking. Of all the elements, wind has the most profound effect on paddlers. In many areas, powerful winds can blow up very suddenly, so it's important to constantly monitor wind conditions. Strong winds can blow kayakers offshore, making headway impossible, or even with a violent gust capsizing a paddler. Weather reports and forecasts are great tools for predicting wind conditions, but as always, the greatest defense is a conservative attitude and a plan that keeps kayaks close to shore and in calm, protected waters.

Waves are another serious hazard. They're most commonly created by wind, although strong currents will also cause formidable waves to build. Handling a kayak in waves is very difficult. Playing in small surf in warm conditions can be incredibly fun, but unless you are 100 percent ready to swim, and appropriately dressed to do so, don't even consider it. In cold water, waves are to be treated with great respect and avoided in favor of calm water or solid ground.

Fog can also seriously affect a kayaker's ability to safely travel on the water. Being enveloped in fog is really eerie and extremely disorienting. It's all too easy to be completely stripped of any sense of direction and hopelessly lost. In many locations, fog is seasonal or occurs in accordance with certain prevailing weather patterns. It may also be more common in the mornings or evenings. Fog can roll in quickly, obscuring landmarks and blotting out all reference points, so be very wary and avoid getting caught out; head for home and hug the shore at the first sign of fog forming.

Rain is no big deal when you're out in a kayak, but thunder and lightning are another matter. Thunder signals the approach of a lightning storm. Lightning is very, very dangerous for anyone out on the water. Bobbing on the surface of the water, a paddler is often the highest point for quite a distance in any direction. This makes you a natural lightning rod. At the first hint of thunder or lightning, get off the water immediately!

Fog can be extremely disorienting and can roll in surprisingly quickly in some areas. If fog is common where you paddle, it's a good idea to always hug the shoreline.

ON WATER TRAFFIC

Sometimes it may seem as if the natural elements are the least of a paddler's worries. In a busy harbor or on a crowded lake, monitoring and avoiding on-water traffic can be a full-time job.

The one essential rule is that "might is right." Just like being a pedestrian or a cyclist, all that matters is avoiding being run over and squashed. Commercially operated boats and ships usually have a regular, established route. They also tend to stick to deeper water and maneuver very predictably, so they're easy to avoid. Even fast-moving floatplanes are very predictable in their landings and takeoffs. No wonder; professionals are driving those crafts!

Generally, it's the amateur sailor's movements that are hard to predict. Powerboats can certainly zigzag at speed unexpectedly, but for the ultimate in erratic navigation, nothing beats the personal watercraft.

By staying close to shore, most serious boat traffic is easily avoided. By remaining in shallow water, you'll be far safer, as a larger vessel couldn't run a kayak down even if it wanted to; it would run aground long before it reached you.

The attitude that it's up to other, faster watercraft to avoid you is a losing philosophy.

When paddling in high traffic areas, it's only prudent to assume that power boats and commercial ships can't see you.

You must proactively make yourself as visible as possible by wearing high-visibility colors and seek out routes and locations that are as empty of boat traffic as possible. Because kayaks are relatively slow moving, there isn't the ability to race away from potential collisions. The emphasis needs be on staying aware of others' movements, and avoidance, because in any collision with another vessel, a kayaker is always likely to come out the loser.

SEA HAZARDS

If you plan to paddle on the sea, you must have an abiding respect for the inherent power and highly dynamic nature of the ocean environment. Conditions can change alarmingly quickly, and wind, waves, fog, or even strong currents can develop in the blink of an eye. As always, staying close to shore and selecting protected paddling locations are your best strategies for having a safe, fun outing. You also need to realize that when conditions start to deteriorate, the best course of action is to get off the water quickly.

Tides cause water levels to rise and fall on the ocean, and this can radically change the shoreline. Low tide can expose sharp, barnacle-covered rocks, cause channels to run dry, or reveal expansive mud flats that can leave you stranded far from the water.

Although magical, the sea is a highly dynamic and powerful environment, and conditions can change alarmingly quickly. If you're going to paddle on the ocean, stick to sheltered waters and gentle beaches, or else take a sea kayaking course on how to stay safe in open water.

High tides may cover beaches, swallowing potential landing or launch sites. Rising water will invariably catch the unwary paddler who leaves an unattended kayak by the shore too long, picking up the boat and floating it away.

Tides also create currents that can be very powerful, and at beaches, waves can cause strong currents called rip currents. Public beaches subject to rip currents are usually well sign-posted, but when in doubt, ask locals and stay close to shore and in sheltered bays and beaches. Avoid headlands and points, as these are magnets for rougher conditions and higher winds.

*A rip current is formed when water that has been pushed up on a beach
by breaking waves is pulled back out by gravity through a concentrated channel.
If you find yourself swimming, these rip currents can be very dangerous.*

If you do find a gentle beach with small waves ideal for a little surf practice, be careful of other beach users. Swimmers and folks body surfing, wading in the shallows, playing on surfboards, riding boogie-boards, or even clinging to inflatable pink seahorses, all have just as much right to frolic in the surf as you do. So keep an eye out for them and be especially careful to avoid collisions with others enjoying the beach.

RIVER HAZARDS

Paddling on lazy rivers is great. A gentle current can help push you on your way downstream, and there's nothing like putting your feet up, catching a few rays, and letting the water do the work.

Current, however, can be a formidable danger. Even a very light current can exert amazing pressure on objects in its path. If you plan to paddle a section of river, be sure to thoroughly investigate everything downstream from your put-in. Changes in elevation, sharp corners, or constricted channels all dramatically increase the speed and power of even the smallest river. Likewise, if another river joins the stream that you're paddling, expect water volume to increase, and the effects of current to become more powerful.

Stationary obstacles in moving water are always potential hazards. While rocks and fallen trees can make navigating difficult, "strainers" are downright dangerous. A strainer is any obstacle that allows water to pass through, but not boats or people. The most common form of strainer is created by boulder sieves, logjams, fallen trees, or dense bush and trees by the banks of a river in flood. Strainers are so dangerous because moving water can sweep you into the impassable obstruction and then the

If you are interested in paddling on more than just a gentle river current,
you'll want to take an introductory whitewater kayaking course.
It will make for a safer, more comfortable experience on the river.

force of the current can hold you pinned in place. If your head is trapped underwater and you are unable to swim to safety, a rescuer will have only seconds to complete a successful rescue.

Foot entrapment is another serious hazard. Many riverbeds consist of a jumble of rocks and other debris. When wading in moving water, should your foot go into a depression or crack, the current may push you off balance, trapping your foot in place. Once again, the force of moving water can make it extremely difficult or even impossible to extricate yourself from this dangerous predicament. The safest strategy for avoiding foot entrapment is simply to always swim when in moving water above knee level. This will mean crawling those last few steps into shore instead of standing up, but a little bump on the knee is better than the possible alternative.

Lastly, avoid all weirs and low head dams like the plague! The hydraulics created at the bottom of these man-made structures can be deceptively powerful and will often make it impossible for a swimmer to escape.

CHAPTER FIVE

KAYAKING ACTIVITIES

PADDLING WITH KIDS • FISHING FROM A KAYAK
SNORKELING FROM A KAYAK • KAYAK CAMPING • KAYAK FITNESS

The single biggest reason that kayaking has become so popular and continues to grow in popularity is that kayaking can offer so many different opportunities. For many, kayaking is a means for getting outside, getting exercise, and spending time with friends and family. But more and more people are learning that kayaks can also be fantastic vehicles for pursuing other interests, such as fishing, diving, snorkeling, camping, and general fitness. Let's have a quick look at some of the most popular kayaking activities.

PADDLING WITH KIDS

Messing about in kayaks with kids can be really fun, but it should go without saying that kids--just like adults--always need to wear PFDs when kayaking. With that in mind, be aware that an adult-sized PFD will not be suitable for children. Lifejackets need to fit properly in order to be effective, and there are many kid-sized PFDs on the market at very affordable prices.

Sit-on-top kayaks, in particular, are great for kids, as there is no chance of swamping the kayak, and they are incredibly versatile when it comes to accommodating children of different ages. Younger kids can sit between their parent's legs, whether on a single or tandem kayak. This position will put both participants' minds at ease. Older kids can sit in the front of a tandem and paddle to their heart's content while the parent controls the kayak from the rear. Sit-on-top kayaks also effectively act as movable floating docks that allow kids to jump and swim from them, and then crawl back on top them as they please. Tandem sit-inside kayaks can also be great for paddling with kids, although it's important to remember that a child's attention span won't be the same as yours, and the youngster may lose interest quickly if all you are doing is paddling forward.

Of course, paddling with kids has the potential of being a trial for everyone involved, but there are a few ways to avoid any on-water ugliness. First of all, don't smother kids with rules or technical paddling advice--let them try it their way. Don't expect kids to enjoy spending extended periods of time quietly sitting in a kayak, or efficiently paddling in rhythm for hours. If your plan is to complete an ambitious three-hour tour of the entire lake shoreline (with minimal pit stops), then a full-on mutiny should also be on your schedule. Kids get bored fast if their curiosity and creativity aren't engaged, so wherever possible let them set the goals and make up the games. Their imaginations will astound you, and in seconds they'll be using a kayak in ways that you never even considered. If you do "need" to cover a certain amount of ground, bribery is always a valid option. Bring small treats along for the ride and you'll be able to keep kids interested and happy for a bit longer.

By positioning the child at the front of the kayak, he can paddle to his heart's content while you can keep your eye on the child and maintain control over the boat.

Sit-on-top kayaks are great for kids as they act like floating docks that allow kids to jump and swim from them.

Although giving kids the freedom to play is important, you should introduce enough structure to ensure that everyone remains safe. Keep a constant eye on all activities and set a few basic guidelines and rules--like always wearing a life jacket, and not crossing clearly defined paddling and swimming boundaries.

In the end, in order to have a good time paddling with kids, you need to accept that it will be a different paddling experience than you might be used to--and there's no reason to fight it. You might as well get in there with the rug rats and have a splashing, goofy, good time yourself.

FISHING FROM A KAYAK

The notion of fishing from a kayak is a relatively new idea for most of us, which is ironic because historically the kayak evolved as a working vessel that was essential to the Inuit for hunting and fishing. More and more people are realizing how well kayaks work as fishing boats. In fact, kayak fishing is the fastest growing market segment within paddle sports. Paddlers are now going fishing, and anglers are going paddling, and it's truly amazing to see the size of fish that are being caught from kayaks.

Why are kayaks so good for fishing? Compared to motorized boats, kayaks are inexpensive, durable, easy to transport, highly maneuverable, and able to operate in

Sit-on-top kayaks are becoming incredibly popular within the fishing world because of the access they offer to untouched fishing spots.

very shallow, rocky, and weed-choked waters--which makes new areas accessible. Even more importantly, kayaks offer the real benefits and satisfaction derived from getting exercise. Kayaks also bring you closer to the water, and to the world below the surface. As your boat glides stealthily through the water, you will undoubtedly find yourself more in tune with, and accepted by, those wily critters beneath you.

Kayaks also have some significant technical advantages over bigger crafts. From a kayak, you can troll silently by simply casting your line, placing your rod in a rod holder, and then paddling (forward or backward) along. When you do catch a fish, your kayak will quickly and naturally turn in whatever direction the fish takes.

Although it is possible to fish from any type of kayak, sit-on-tops have become the favorite of anglers, and manufacturers have responded to the demand with fishing-specific features such as rod holders, paddle clips, live-bait wells, holding tanks, and even camouflage color schemes. The reason sit-on-top kayaks are preferred for fishing is that in the case of a capsize, re-entry is not a major ordeal. Sit-on-tops also provide the most versatility when it comes to fishing position. You can sit sideways with your legs over the side of the boat as if you were on a dock. You can even stand up in some models.

If you're interested in learning to fish from a kayak, there are a couple of books on the subject that are worth checking out. There are also kayak fishing guide services in some areas. The great thing about kayak fishing, though, is that all you need

Sit-on-top kayaks can be outfitted with fishing accessories such as rod holders, paddle clips, and holding tanks.

Sit-on-top kayaks provide great platforms for both diving and snorkeling. They have enough room to carry your equipment and are very easy to re-enter on the water.

to do it is a valid fishing license, a safety-conscious attitude, and the desire to try something new.

SNORKELING FROM A KAYAK

When we talk about using a kayak as a vehicle for other activities, snorkeling and diving are the perfect examples. Sit-on-top kayaks are great platforms for doing both, as they will easily carry all the gear that is required. Some boats even have wells molded-in that are specifically designed for carrying an air tank. Sit-on-tops are also very easy to re-enter from the water and provide excellent stability when climbing aboard. In fact, sit-on-tops act very much like floating docks. For snorkeling, a common approach is to use an ankle tether that attaches a leash from your leg to the kayak. This allows you to cruise around as you please, with your boat trailing along behind like a faithful hound. Keeping the boat close like this also gives you the option of taking a break and hanging out on the side of your boat for a rest.

KAYAK CAMPING

There's nothing quite like getting away for a night out under the stars, and doing it in a kayak is sweet. No motor disturbs the silence, and the gentle rhythm of paddling helps other worldly concerns melt away, leaving your mind focused on the simpler tasks of pitching the tent, fluffing your sleeping bag, and roasting a few marshmallows.

The best kayaks for overnight trips are sit-inside kayaks that have separate, waterproof compartments that are accessed through hatches. Of course, the bigger your kayak, the more room you'll have for gear.

When packing your boat, there are a few things to keep in mind, as your gear selection and how you distribute it within the kayak can have a profound effect on how your boat handles and how comfortable you'll be on the trip. As a general rule, you'll want to pack the heaviest items at the bottom of the boat and as close to the center as possible. Keeping weight low will increase stability, whereas strapping heavy items onto the deck will make you very unstable. You also need to pack with the assumption that your bags could end up floating in the water. Having some of your equipment get wet won't be a big deal, but clothing and sleeping gear clearly need to stay dry. Wrapping this stuff in a couple of heavy-duty garbage bags can do the trick, but dry bags are the surest way to keep it all safe from getting wet. Dry bags are exactly what they sound like--waterproof sacks with a special roll-top closure that prevents any water from getting in.

Kayaks are great vehicles for camping trips. Many sit-inside kayaks even have separated waterproof compartments for carrying gear, and have enough room to bring those luxurious items that you might leave behind on a backpacking trip.

One of the great things about kayak camping is that most kayaks that you would use for the purpose have enough storage room to take more gear than you could ever pile on your back. This lets you bring those luxurious camping items that you might leave behind on a backpacking trip.

KAYAK FITNESS

Kayaking--while being a great way to get outside and explore your local waterways, bird watch, fish, or camp--is also a wonderful way to get exercise. In fact, more and more people are looking to kayaking as an alternative, or a complement, to other fitness activities such as biking or jogging. Many fitness enthusiasts like to get exercise each and every day, and kayaking is a great addition to other training regimens, especially since it's one of the few outdoor activities that really focuses the work on the upper body. Another great thing about kayaking is that it does not inflict the same type of pounding on the body that running or jogging does. This helps avoid many of the common overuse injuries, and makes kayaking the perfect choice for people with knee or hip issues.

For fitness paddling, any boat will do the trick, although a narrower kayak will glide through the water more efficiently and allow you to go faster. Of course, this doesn't really make much difference unless you're racing, and there is a real cost for the added speed. As a kayak gets narrower it becomes less stable. Olympic sprint paddlers actually use boats as narrow as eighteen inches at their widest point, which is almost half the width of some recreational kayaks. Simply establishing a balanced sitting position on one of these kayaks is a major challenge for most people!

If you're interested in paddling for fitness, ask around at your local outdoor store or paddling shop to see if there are any programs of that sort in your area. As kayaking for fitness has become more popular, there's been a sharp rise in the number of informal and fun races that have popped up around the country. Some clubs even race for fun on a weekly basis, and these laid-back events provide an excellent opportunity for getting to know other paddlers with similar interests.

Kayaking is quickly becoming one of the most popular summer fitness activities as it is low impact, provides a great workout, and can be done virtually anywhere.

GLOSSARY OF TERMS

Back Band A padded band of material that provides back support.

Backrest Rigid seat back (often padded and adjustable in angle and height) that provides back support.

Bilge Bottom of the inside of a boat.

Bilge Pump Device for pumping water out of a boat.

Bow The front of a boat.

Bowline Cord attached to the front of the boat; useful for towing or tying the boat to a dock.

Bulkhead A waterproof wall that divides the interior of a kayak, creating flotation and storage areas.

Bungee The elastic lines used to secure gear on the deck of a kayak.

Cargo The items transported in a boat.

Coaming The lip around the cockpit that allows the attachment of a sprayskirt.

Cockpit The seating area in a kayak.

Deck The top of a kayak.

Deck Line Rope or shock-cord attached to a kayak's deck; used for securing items on deck or to facilitate grabbing the boat.

Drain Plug A stopper mounted in the stern that can be removed to drain a kayak.

Dry bag A waterproof bag that seals (usually with a roll-top system) to keep water out.

Feather The twist or offset between the two blades of a kayak paddle.

Float Bags Airtight bags that are secured inside a kayak to displace water and create flotation.

Foot Wells Molded recesses in the deck of a kayak where the paddler puts the feet.

Handles Carrying toggles found at the bow and stern of a kayak.

Hatch The opening into a cargo compartment in a kayak.

Hull The bottom of a boat.

Kayak A watercraft propelled by a double-bladed paddle.

Leg Leash A tether that ties a kayak to the paddler.

Life Jacket A flotation device worn like a vest.

Paddle Kayak paddles are double-bladed devices for propelling the boat. Canoe paddles have only one blade.

Paddle Leash Tether that attaches a paddle to a kayak.

Perimeter Lines Cords that run around the edges of the deck on a kayak, making the boat easier to grab.

PFD Personal Floatation Device; see "Life Jacket."

Portage To carry a kayak or canoe overland.

Put In The location where you start your trip.

Rip Tide/Current Strong current on a beach, created by waves--potentially very dangerous.

Rod Holder Device for holding a fishing rod.

Roof Rack System of two bars that mount to the roof of a vehicle for transporting kayaks and other loads.

Rudder Foot-controlled steering mechanism mounted at the back of a kayak.

Scupper A hole that goes through a boat allowing water to drain off the deck back into the sea/lake/river.

Skeg A blade or fin that drops into the water to help a kayak go straight.

Spraydeck/Sprayskirt A nylon or neoprene skirt worn around the waist; attaches to the kayak coaming to keep water out of the boat.

Stern Back of the boat.

Takeout The location where your paddling trip ends.

Tank Well Molded-in recess in a kayak designed to carry a diver's oxygen tank.

Tidal Rip Strong current created by changes in tide height.

Tie-Down A strap or rope used to secure a kayak to the roof of a vehicle.

Thigh Straps After-market accessory that attaches to a sit-on-top to allow the kayak to be gripped by the paddler's legs.

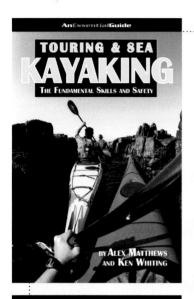
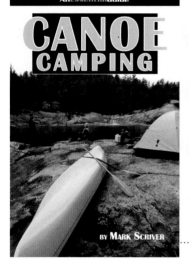